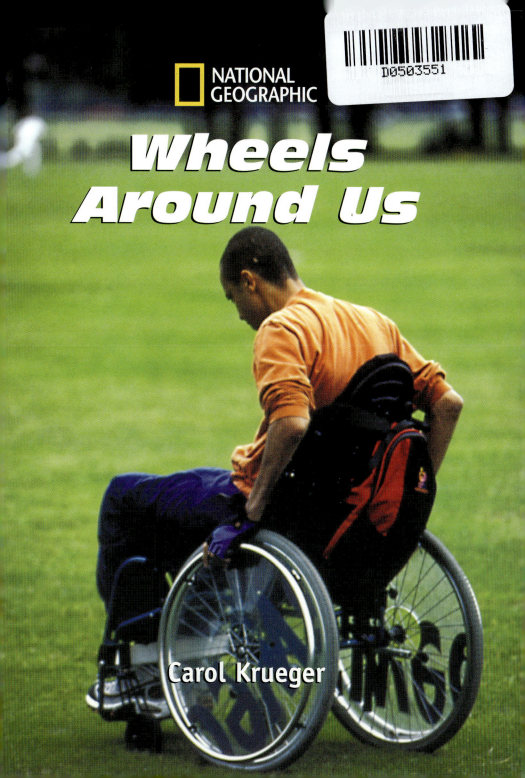

NATIONAL GEOGRAPHIC

Wheels Around Us

Carol Krueger

Contents

What are Wheels?

Many things have wheels. Wheels help people work, travel, carry loads, and have fun.

Wheels turn around in circles. The center of a wheel is connected to a bar called an **axle**. The wheel spins around the axle.

A wheel and an axle together are a **simple machine**. Some axles are attached to two wheels, and some are attached to only one wheel.

A bicycle wheel has its own axle.

These two wheels on a skateboard are joined by one axle.

3

Wheels of the Past

Nobody knows who invented the wheel. Thousands of years ago, people used **rollers** made from tree trunks to help move heavy things. They placed rollers beneath heavy objects so they could be moved easily.

rollers

The first wheels and axles to be developed were made of solid wood. These wheels were heavy. Carts with wheels, like the one shown on this page, couldn't move very quickly.

spokes

Later in history, people made wheels with rods called **spokes**. These wheels were still strong, but they were much lighter than solid wheels. Wheels with spokes helped carts move quickly.

Wheels and Tires

Today, many wheels have rubber tires. Wheels with tires are used on many kinds of vehicles. The tire fits tightly around the rim of the wheel. Usually tires need to be filled with air. Tires also need a textured surface that will not slip and slide on the ground. This surface is the tread of the tire. Like all wheels, wheels with tires have axles.

A car has two axles—
a front axle and a rear axle.

tire

tread

rim

Some wheelchairs have air-filled tires. Some have solid tires. Each wheel on a wheelchair has its own axle.

Airplanes have wheels so they can move along the ground. Their wheels help them roll to take off and land. To lift off the ground into the air, an airplane has to travel very fast down the runway. The wheels roll smoothly so that the engines can move the plane fast enough to lift off.

Trucks have to carry heavy loads, often a long way. They need strong, large wheels. Some trucks have wheels that are bigger than the driver!

Sometimes long trucks have many wheels. This truck has 52 wheels!

Wheels For Fun

Some wheels help us have fun.

Many people enjoy inline skating. Inline skates have hard plastic wheels. Each wheel has its own axle.

Roller skates have been used for more than 200 years. In 1760, a man named Joseph Merlin made a pair of roller skates and wore them to a party. Unfortunately, he didn't put stoppers on his skates. When he skated into the party, he couldn't stop. He crashed into a mirror! Many skates today have stoppers so we can slow down or stop as needed.

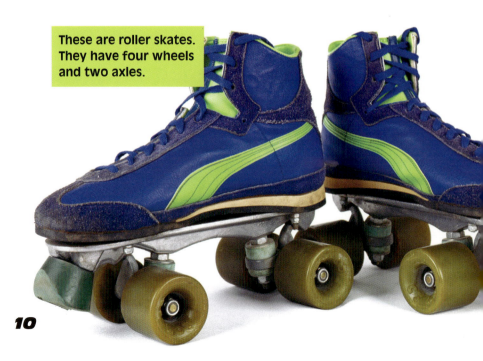

These are roller skates. They have four wheels and two axles.

You can have fun skating by yourself. There are also other kinds of wheels that you can ride on for fun with lots of people. On a Ferris wheel, people sit in seats on the rim of the wheel. The Ferris wheel spins around a strong axle in the middle. This special kind of wheel was invented in 1893 by George Ferris for the Chicago World's Fair. Ferris wheels are still popular today, and some of them are enormous.

Ferris wheel

Where else would you see a big wheel at a carnival? The carousel, or merry-go-round, is also a large wheel! The seats are on top of a platform, which is a wheel that rotates just above the ground.

carousel

Wheels in Water

Not all wheels are used on land. Some wheels help people travel on water, too.

Paddle boats use large wheels to move them through the water. Paddles are attached to the wheels. When the wheels turn, the paddles push the boat along. Some paddle boats are called paddle steamers. The engine uses steam from boiling water to make the wheels move.

Today, paddle steamers are mostly used by tourists.

paddle wheel

Water bikes also use special wheels to help them move through the water. These wheels are hollow, so they float. Ridges on the wheels help push the bike along. But the energy needed to turn the wheels comes from the person pedaling!

Making Things with Wheels

Not all wheels help us carry loads or move. Other wheels help us make things.

A pottery wheel is flat and spins very fast. People can shape wet clay on a pottery wheel very quickly using their hands and simple tools. Some pottery wheels use electricity to make them turn.

A spinning wheel uses several different sized wheels to help people spin wool. The wheels move when a person pushes his or her feet down on a special lever called a **treadle**. The treadle makes the big wheel spin and also controls how fast the wheel turns. The big wheel makes the smaller wheels turn.

treadle

Pottery wheels and spinning wheels have been used since ancient times. The pottery wheel may have been one of the first wheels ever invented!

Wheels Everywhere

We can find wheels everywhere around us. Some wheels are part of another machine, and some don't really look like wheels. We use wheels and axles every day and sometimes don't even know it.

Do your doors have doorknobs that you turn? A doorknob has two wheels and an axle. When the doorknob is turned, it turns the axle, which pulls the latch in.

wheel

latch

Some people have special reels for their garden hoses. The hose winds around the axle. This makes storing the hose neater. It is also easy to unwind and rewind the hose on the axle.

Sometimes people use eggbeaters to help mix food. An eggbeater's blades and handle are attached to a wheel. The handle turns the wheel, which makes the blades turn. This mixes up the food.

Wheels Turning Wheels

Sometimes one wheel helps to turn another wheel. Special wheels called **cogwheels** have pieces that resemble teeth around the rim. These pieces are called cogs. The cogs fit between one another on a cogwheel. So when one cogwheel turns it makes the others turn, too.

cogwheel

There are cogwheels inside some clocks. They help make the clock's hands move around to show the time.

Pulleys

Pulleys are another kind of simple machine that uses wheels. Pulley wheels have grooves that a rope, chain, or cable fits into. When you pull the rope, the pulley lifts things up.

A flagpole uses a pulley to raise and lower the flag. The flag is attached to a long loop of thin rope that fits into the groove of a small pulley wheel. When you pull one side of the rope loop down, the other side goes up. The flag goes up, too.

Ski lifts use pulleys to transport people up and down mountains.

GLOSSARY

Axle — a bar or rod that is fixed to a wheel

Cogwheel — a wheel with teeth called cogs

Pulley — a simple machine using a wheel and a rope

Roller — a tree log used to help roll objects along the ground

Simple Machine — a simple device that helps us do work. There are six simple machines: a wheel and axle; a pulley; a lever; a wedge; a screw; and a ramp

Spokes — a strong bar or rod that goes from the center of the wheel to the rim

Treadle — a special kind of pedal or lever that you move with your foot